FROM HOPING TO HAVING

AFFIRMATION BOOKLET

The Ultimate Law of Attraction Affirmation Booklet

JULIE POOLE

BSc; SQHP.

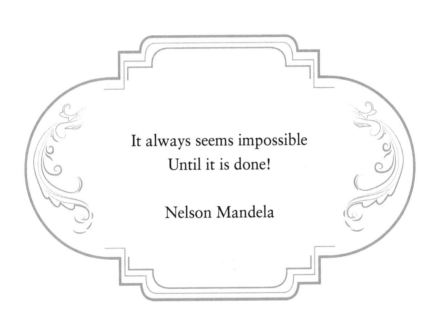

It always seems impossible
Until it is done!

Nelson Mandela

CONTENTS

PART 1 – REMEMBER

PART TWO: RESET

PART 3 – RECEIVE

INTRODUCTION

This is an affirmation booklet to help you create your greatest life, a life which is joyful and abundant in all areas. These affirmations will help you to be all that you can be and have all that you desire to have. This is the ultimate law of attraction affirmation booklet!

This booklet has been created alongside my book, 'From Hoping to Having - The 3 'R's to Create Your Best Life – Remember; Reset; Receive' and follows its chapters and the three 'Rs'. If you are reading this in conjunction with the book, 'From Hoping to Having', at the end of each chapter, use the affirmations in this booklet for the same chapter to strengthen your manifestation and help you achieve your goals quicker and easier. You do not need to read the book alongside these affirmations; they will still aid you in your creation of your greatest life.

As in the full book, this affirmation booklet is in three

parts. Remember is Part One and is key in creating the life that you truly desire in order for you to move from the hoping to the having. It is all about your power. As you remember and step into your power, you will begin to create the life that you really want. Affirmations to support your power are in this first section.

Reset is the second part; with affirmations to help you alter, amend, and change your current thinking and release blocks so that you can align fully with all that you desire. Part three is the receiving. Affirmations which support you in moving that which you desire into your reality.
It is important that you *feel the feelings* of the affirmations, and not just speak the words aloud or in your head. Connect your emotions and energy to the words and really step into the feeling of them as you use the affirmations.

Use this booklet daily until you move From Hoping to Having.

With love and blessings,
Julie Poole

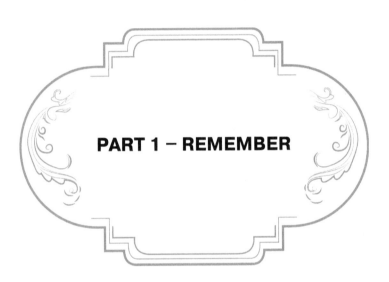

PART 1 – REMEMBER

1

AFFIRMATIONS FOR ALIGNING WITH YOUR CREATIVE FORCE

I am a powerful creator.

I am All That I Am.

I am a synergy. I am made up of many parts and the sum of those parts is greater than each of the individual parts.

I am a spark of consciousness in the vastness of universal consciousness.

I see and know my incredible magnificence and light.

I am a being of incredible light, of immense power, fortitude, and inspiration.

I know my great worth. I am worthy.

I am able to be more of who I truly am. I am able to receive what I truly want.

I know and remember my power. I create from a position of power. I manifest all I desire.

I am manifesting and creating healthy, happy relationships and connections.

I am creating a life of ease, with freedom from fear and worry.

I am secure financially and feel secure financially.

I follow my passions, my dreams, and I create new experiences.

I desire a healthy and energised body. I am aligned with balance, harmony, vitality. I am thriving in my body, mind, and soul.

I desire happiness. I am invoking a beautiful light within and around me of happiness. My heart lifts, and my spirit soars into happiness.

I am creating all that I desire.

I have the power to create the life that I want. I am Source personified, glorified, and much revered.

I am all that I am. All that I am is divine. All that I am is love. I am the light. I am the love. I am a spark of consciousness that separated from Source, and then returned to Source, expanded. I am what grew Source, expanded Source. Source is there because of me. Source loves me.

I am one with All That Is. I am the light; I am the love that grew from the light. I am the power.

I am the light, the love, the power, and the way. I am that spark of consciousness. I hold power, I hold force, I hold love, and I hold light.

I am open to my own innate inner knowing and my intuition.

I am now remembering my power and allowing it to become one with me.

I have a two-way relationship with Source: a relationship that has mutual love, mutual respect, and mutual benefit.

2

AFFIRMATIONS FOR ALIGNING WITH THE LAW OF ATTRACTION

God is good. God is all powerful. God is love. I am God personified. I am good. I am powerful. I am love.

Source, the 'All That Is' does not judge me, or condemn me and neither does Source parent me, grow me, or answer my prayers. I do it. I create my reality; I create my expansion. I also create my restriction, my reduction, my pain, or my pleasure. This is my free will, this is my power, this is The Truth. I choose now to create a wonderful life going forward.

I have absolute free will. Free will is absolute. I have free will to create, just as Source does, because I am a part of Source.

My greatest power is my 'I AM'. My 'I AM Presence'. My God-self, my creative force, my divine intelligence within my being. I am activating that within me which is all knowing. I AM calling upon the I AM to come forward and assist me with that which helps be more of who I am, on all levels.

I am aligning myself to my greatest force, my greatest power – my creative power! I allow my human self, my ego self to step back and allow my 'I AM' to come forward.

I have total freedom. I have free dominion. I have freedom to decide, to choose, to construct, to go with or against the flow, to feel into what feels good for me and what feels bad. I choose, from this point forward, to bring into my life that which feels good.

I create, I choose, I decide. I am free.

I am the creator of my framework. I am the creator of my reality. I know my power. I feel it, I act on it, I create from it, I use it, and I allow it.

My 'I AM' is within my cellular structure of my physical body, within my thoughts, both consciously and subconsciously; within my emotions and feeling; within my energy and within every particle of my energy. My I Am is within the whole of who I am, and who I am yet to become. I now activate the 'I AM'. I am allowing the divine intelligence within me to come forward and assist me. I AM now allowing my I AM to guide my life.

I am surrendering my entire being to that which I truly am - my divinity within. I am utilising this divine power for whatever I wish.

I AM calling upon the divine intelligence within my being to come forward. I allow all the answers to flow to me, empowering me into appropriate action.

Mighty I AM Presence within, come forth.

I am now utilising my mighty I AM power. I feel it, I am comfortable with it, I am one with it.

My thoughts become things. My thoughts work powerful for my benefit.

I easily access all that is not in my highest good or in my best interests and I am able to easily, and safely, clear and release it.

I choose to align with abundance, peace, health, wealth, love, prosperity, ease, and flow, and to know and experience my full power and potential.

I AM all that I AM. All that I AM is now aligned with my divine self.

I seek to be healthy, happy, wealthy, successful, loving. I am aligned with these desires.

I remember, I am God in human form, and I am creator.

I am aligned with success right now. Any part of my being that is not aligned with success, I command it to come forward now for peaceful resolution. I have the ability and the power to do this.

I am releasing all blocks and all that does not serve me, safely and gently, now.

I realise and accept that the ability to create is innate within my being. It is part of who I am and who I will always be.

My beliefs work for me, with me, to assist me in being all I can be and in accessing and allowing my full potential.

3

AFFIRMATIONS FOR POSITIVITY

I am a mass of energy, vibrating at speed. My positive energy enables my intuition to flow, my inner guidance system to be turned on fully and for me to manifest and create my reality in a consciously positive way.

Raising my vibration enables me to live an abundant life. I am now raising my vibration into my best self.

I feel extremely positive, and know instinctively what is good for me, right for me, best for me.

I am limitless with boundless possibilities and can bridge the gap in the 'hoping' and in the 'having' easily.

I easily identify what reduces my vibration and what lifts it.

I notice the way the energy grows and expands.

I identify and observe my energy, my body, my emotions, and my thoughts.

I am in a state of positivity with heightened awareness. I feel and am aware of my emotions. I sense my body in a very active way. I am aware of other people's energy, and of the energy of the environment around me.

I am connected with my higher self and my own energy, feeling my vibration, and aligning myself with peace, joy, and gratitude.

I have access to, and am aware of universal consciousness and All That Is.

I am empowered, uplifted, enlightened, with endless possibilities before me. There is joy and excitement in my body and in my heart.

Life is open, I am open, all is well.

I am energised in my physical being. I walk tall, shoulders back, feeling good, a smile on my face and joy in my heart.

I avoid low vibrational, negative situations as much as I can within my environment. I prioritise being in a higher vibration which benefits me.

I choose to stay in a light, loving energy.

I AM a being of light and I retain my lightest, highest possible, most positive vibration.

My first relationship is with myself. I focus on loving myself, respecting myself, protecting myself. I have healthy, loving boundaries with myself. I am positive with myself.

Thank you for helping me to stay in a wonderfully high vibration when I am around negative people and situations. Thank you for helping me to see their pain, and to show compassion and care to them, whilst I remain in my own place of love.

I am here on this exciting journey to my best life. I am choosing wisely which vibrations I expose myself to.

4

AFFIRMATIONS FOR UNIVERSAL HELP

I have access to heal my wounds and limitations, to be the healthiest, happiest version of myself, and to get to that place easily.

I call upon assistance from the universe in the release of resistance, allowing the abundance of energy to flow to and through me. I am aligning my body and mind to know all it can be.

I am what I believe, and what I believe creates my reality.

There is an outside field of help available to me if I choose it. It is alright if I choose only to access my own power within.

My intuition is my internal navigation system which connects all parts of me. I feel my intuition. I listen to it. I allow it to guide me.

I am aligned with ease and acceptance, power, and joy and all that the universe can provide.

I am connected to my team of spiritual beings that surround and assist me, continuously. My angels, loved ones, guides, elders, ancestors, and higher beings of light are always with me and always ready to help me.

My higher self and my I AM are my greatest power. They are available to me always and continuously.

I am calling upon my spiritual team to assist me in creating my greatest life.

I ask and it is given. I receive all universal and high vibrational help, willingly. All help is available to me from the universe on multiple levels, supporting my greatest good.

5

AFFIRMATIONS FOR PERSONAL POWER

I have incredible human will, determination, self-belief, and self-mastery. I am so powerful!

I have incredible self-belief. I have total faith in myself. I know and feel that I have enormous capacity for achievement.

I recall, easily the times of personal pride and happiness that I have experienced. I relive that pride and am fully aware of my many wins. I feel the feelings of the incredible satisfaction, achievement, pride, and happiness that I felt then. My power is being recalled. I have power to achieve. I have power to grow. I have power to accomplish. I can do it! I can do anything! I can do anything I set my mind to.

My power belongs to me, and only me.

I am so powerful.

I have power. I have achieved wonderful things before. I can and will achieve wonderful things again. I did it before and I will do again.

I praise myself often. I deserve praise and encouragement.

I stand in my magnificence. I know my worth. I am amazing.

I can do, be and have anything that I set my mind to.

I am unlimited.

I believe in me.

I am proud of me.

I have understood, claimed, and stepped into my personal power, spiritual power, and my I AM power. I am powerful.

6

AFFIRMATIONS FOR CREATING A LIFE OF ABUNDANCE

I know my power. I know my worth. I know my importance and my divine right to be all that I choose to be. I allow all that I choose to flow to me.

I am energy vibrating. I resonate at a frequency which draws to me like frequencies. I attract positive frequencies from this moment forward.

I am my beliefs. I do not get what I want, I get what I am. My beliefs now support me and serve my highest good.

My beliefs are an energetic resonance which mirror my truth. I get what I believe. I now see the truth from a higher perspective. My beliefs now work for my highest good. All false beliefs fall away now.

I am aligned with freedom and ease.

I desire loving connections. I am now aligned with loving connections.

The Law of Attraction will bring to me that which I resonate with. I now resonate with wealth and ease. I choose wealth, ease, and flow in my life.

I desire health, vitality, and energy. I am energised, healthy and full of vitality.

I desire to be in the energy of abundance of time. I have plenty of time. I am time rich. I have so much time. Time is abundant!

I am God personified. I am All That Is. I am the I AM. I am special. I am important.

I desire more from and with life.

I am aligned with the feeling of that which I desire. I am aligned with the feeling of what my life feels like to have wealth show up in it – it feels easy, content. I am easy and content.

Wealth creates freedom. I am free now. I am free. I feel the feelings of freedom, ease, and contentment, now.

I love, respect and value money. I am worthy of money. I am worthy of all good things.

I am a vibrational match to the things I desire.

I feel free. I am secure. I am empowered. I am safe. I am content. I am unlimited.

I AM free from all limitations. I am unlimited. I release all that holds me back and align with all that I desire.

Show me how good life can be.

7

AFFIRMATIONS FOR BELIEVING

I believe in myself. I believe in my power. I believe I have a divine right to abundance in all areas of my life.

I feel the feelings of that which I align with. I feel free. I feel safe. I feel secure. I am free. I am safe. I am secure.

I feel abundant. I Am abundant. My life is rich in so many ways.

I am successful now. I feel successful. I have achieved so many successes in my life already and I am excited to experience more.

My beliefs support me in my present moment. All beliefs that are outdated and no longer serve me, I release now, safely, easily, and gently.

I am easily able to identity thoughts which do not serve me.

I am rich now. My life holds so much richness, in so many ways, it is beautiful.

I am easily able to neutralise and delete thoughts that do not serve and support me. All my thoughts serve my highest good and my greatest life.

I am healthy. I am increasingly healthy. My body is a healing machine capable of incredible balance and wellbeing. I am stepping into full healing now.

I believe I deserve and can attain a wonderful job which is fulfilling, enjoyable and that pays me well.

I am aligned with my own power to create a wonderful life for myself.

I feel really good around money. I am aligned with money. I am ready to have money show up in my life in greater quantities.

I am aligned with money. I am aligned with wealth. I am aligned with ease.

My reaction to money arriving in my life in greater quantities is joy, freedom, excitement, pleasure, and gratitude.

I receive compliments with grace, appreciation, and gratitude.

I AM wealthy now.

I am aligned with all good things. I allow myself to receive all good things gratefully and gracefully, joyously, and happily.

I feel the feelings of freedom and choice, power and security, happiness, and joy. Great wealth brings me freedom and choice, power and security, happiness, and joy. I feel gratitude and appreciation for money. I value money. I respect money.

I respect and value money. I meet my own needs first, and then I gift to others.

I cannot align with abundance for someone else, only myself. I am aligned with abundance and prosperity for me, my life, and my world, now.

I attract money to myself. I receive it. I am grateful for it. I am in the joy of it. I allow it to benefit me. I share the wealth with others in the service of others.

I feel the feelings of money coming into my life and feel so much gratitude. I feel love, I feel life, and life is now showing me just how good it can be.

8

AFFIRMATIONS FOR ALLOWING

I allow all my needs to always be met in abundant, prosperous, luxurious ways. I have more than enough to meet my basic needs and also my pleasurable needs. Money brings me joy and happiness.

I desire and deserve a life which is rich in its pleasure and joy. I allow the flow of pleasure and joy in my life at all times.

I am easily able to access and allow the flow of unlimited abundance. I feel so good as I access unlimited abundance!

I am aligned with limitless abundance in all areas of my life. I welcome and appreciate limitless abundance.

Limitless abundance is available to me now.

I am worthy of great avalanches of abundance. I am deserving. I know this to be true in every fibre of my being. I allow all good things to come to me now.

I step into my I AM and know my power and worth. I am commanding the Mighty I AM to show me and align me with my incredible worth. I have an absolute right to abundance. I deserve all good things.

All good things come to me now. All good things flow easily and readily into my energy and life.

Money flows to me easily and readily and stays present in my life, always. There is a constant flow of abundance into my life at all times. I allow this great flow at all times.

I have unlimited time to achieve and accomplish all that I desire to do. Time works with me. There is an abundance of time which I access easily.

I easily allow myself small and large pleasures. I deserve and desire pleasurable experiences.

Money comes to me in multiple ways, through multiple streams, in a constant and continual flow of ease.

I am easily able to access the bank of the universe whenever I choose. The universe is abundant. All abundance is readily available to me.

I am thankful for the universe supporting me.

I am completely free in all areas of my life. I have freedom. I am freedom. My life is free and unlimited, unrestricted, and free flowing.

I am easily able to reprioritise my life. I am easily able to examine my commitments, responsibilities, boundaries.

I let go of all that does not serve me. I always see alternatives. Ways will be shown to me for all options, choices, and resources when I call when I open up to them. I am open to all options for my best life and in my highest good.

Money provides security, safety, and stability to me. I value and appreciate money in all aspects of my life.

I am open to guidance, signs, and synchronicities. I listen to my heart, my intuition, and my desire for more ease. I allow all that is good to come to me. I act, where and when I feel guided to act.

The Universe creates opportunities for me. I am aligned with abundance in all areas of my life. I am aligned and open to opportunities to create greater abundance.

New people come into my life and open doors to other new opportunities which support my greatest life.

My life is easier and easier every day in every way.

I trust that the Universe has ways to make things come about. I trust and believe. Opportunities which benefit me come to me now.

I am open to abundance in the form of refunds, free gifts, and surprises. Money flows easily and readily to me and creates the ease I seek.

I am aligned with freedom.

I now see opportunities that were previously hidden from my view. Opportunities which support my best life.

PART TWO: RESET

9

AFFIRMATIONS FOR CLEAR BOUNDARIES

My boundary is what I judge to be acceptable or unacceptable.

I decide where my boundaries are.

I am now able to examine and amend my boundaries from a perspective of freedom and love.

I am now able to examine and amend my boundaries from the perspective of my own greater good.

I examine and amend my boundaries from the perspective of my own inner peace.

My boundaries are based on a foundation of love and freedom.

I am free to set my own boundaries.

My boundaries are there for me, and only me. They are my boundary with myself, and only myself. My boundary is my line. I have free will to move my boundaries where I will.

I treat others with love and respect.

My boundary with myself is my moral compass. My boundary is my line.

I respect others and show respect to others.

My boundary is for me only. I treat myself with respect.

I choose to treat others with respect.

I choose to remove myself from other people's disrespect, or to ignore it. I let go of the outcome.

I let go of expecting another to treat me the same way that I would treat them. They are them. I am me.

I no longer react negatively to others, I simply observe. As I observe, I observe my own judgement and easily remove it.

I remain in a peaceful place within my being when others show me disrespect.

I allow others to be in the space that they are in from a place of loving compassion.

I am holding my own space. I am holding my own power. I am disallowing another's behaviour and actions to impact me. I remain where I am in my own energy. I am lovingly compassionate with others.

I allow each person to have their own levels, standards, and boundaries, and for me to have my own.

I live the way of peaceful serenity, allowing myself to be at peace and remain at peace, despite others' behaviour and actions around me.

I am allowing all to be who they are, including myself, with the freedom to choose, always.

I stand firm in my convictions of my own boundaries.

I am willing to assert my boundaries. I am choosing to make a commitment to myself.

I am showing myself and others that it is permissible to say no, that it is permissible to put my own needs and my own well-being first, and that they have the option to do the same, should they choose to.

10

AFFIRMATIONS TO RELEASE RESPONSIBILITIES

I am responsible for myself and only myself.

I let go of needing to fix, sort, repair or take responsibility for other people's problems.

I am able to assist, support and help others when it feels right for me to do so.

Other people's issues and problems are theirs. Mine are mine. I am able to support and guide only. I release all expectation and responsibility for the outcome.

I am easily able to access alternative resources.

I am responsible for my own wellbeing.

I let go of being overly involved with others. I release taking upon responsibility for them and of their problems, issues, and concerns.

I absolve myself of responsibility for others.

I take ownership of my own responsibilities and allow others to have theirs.

I am able to be helpful, kind, and thoughtful. I am able to offer support, assistance, help, guidance, and my time to others.

I offer assistance to others when it feels right for me to do so, without harming myself in any way.

I let go of other people's problem. I have a choice to assist the other or to let go and allow them to remedy their own problems.

I release responsibility for someone else's outcome.

I accept that others have their own path, their own choices, their own mistakes, their own learning, and their own development.

I release being an enabler. I release the need or desire to assist or encourage others in being helpless. I release disempowering others. I release this now.

I am responsible for me, and only me. I am responsible for my choices and options, decisions, and outcomes.

I let go of taking personal responsibility for another's life, well-being, or happiness.

I hold loving connections with others without assuming responsibility for them, without being overwhelmed by them or their problems. I am releasing responsibility for others now. I hold healthy boundaries which support me.

I regularly check in with myself and ask myself, what is mine and what is theirs. I assume responsibility for myself only.

I assist others, rather than enable. I support, rather than disempower. I allow others to take full responsibility for themselves, including the consequences, mistakes, triumphs, dramas, and issues.

AFFIRMATIONS TO RELEASE COMMITMENTS

I set healthy boundaries for myself and my life.

I am reunited with my own sense of personal responsibility.

I let go of the need to fix and be responsible for others.

I am able to let go of commitments that harm my wellbeing and freedoms.

I easily examine what time I have available to help others.

I seek out additional help to meet the gap in what others need and what I can comfortably give.

There are multiple resources available to me and to others.

I let go of any guilt which arises when I say no.

I am able to research available help from multiple sources.

I am able and willing to reach out for help from others. I allow all available help to come to me now.

I am open to receive help and trust.

I am able to review my commitments. I give myself full permission to change, alter, and amend my commitments if they no longer serve me.

I am easily able to bring my attention into my own life and set firmer boundaries that support and protect me. I protect and value my time, my energy, and my life.

I am easily able to ask myself if my commitment is working for me.

I can change my mind and withdraw or reduce the help and support that I offer to another, at any time.

I take appropriate action.

I hand back responsibility to the other for them to meet their own commitments.

I easily make the changes that I seek.

I question myself as to whether I am supporting or enabling another and take appropriate action to make changes which support my wellbeing.

I question if my commitment is good for me or overwhelming me and take appropriate action to make changes which support my wellbeing.

I ensure that if I do not sacrifice my own happiness for another. I easily and comfortably take appropriate action to make changes which support my wellbeing.

There is always another way, another door, another option when I choose to look for it. I see all available options.

I regularly ask myself if my boundaries, responsibilities, and commitments serve me, or hinder me. I take appropriate action to make changes which support my wellbeing.

I am able to create change where it feels right for me to do so.

AFFIRMATIONS FOR MY OWN APPROVAL

I am able to rely on myself.

I seek my own approval.

I allow others to disagree with me and to withhold approval.

I am able to trust my own inner guidance.

I am good enough, safe enough, confident enough in myself and seek only my own approval from my inner knowing.

I let go of judgement and disapproval from others.

The only judgement and approval that matters, is my own.

My feelings are my feedback mechanism from my soul and will tell me all I need. I listen and trust my soul.

I am important. I have always been important. My dreams and goals matter.

My soul yearns to experience what it desires. I listen to my soul and inner guidance over and above all and everyone else, always.

I am taking my power back by seeking my own approval over others. I have every right to take my power back. My power is mine. My power belongs to me.

I matter, my needs matter, my desires matter, my opinion matters, my inner calling matters, my path matters, my choices matter, my heart matters.

I let go of the need for approval from others and accept that we may have a differing of opinions and that it is okay to disagree. I allow the disapproval of others and let go of trying to change it.

I follow my own guidance and let go of others influence over me.

The only approval I need is my own. My own inner guidance, my own moral compass, my own sense of right and wrong. I am now aligned with my own approval.

13

AFFIRMATIONS FOR SUCCESS

I am happy and comfortable to be seen.

I am happy and comfortable to be noticed.

I am happy and comfortable to be visible in my success.

I let go of all fear of becoming power hungry.

I let go of fear of becoming a control freak.

I let go of fear of becoming famous.

I let go of fear of becoming greedy.

I am comfortable with success.

I let go of fear of failure.

I embrace success in all its forms.

I accept that failures may happen. I see failures as growth opportunities.

I let go of fear of growth or change. Change is there to expand me into the best version of myself. I grow and change all the time.

I allow life to be free flowing and free forming.

I experience success. I am successful.

I enjoy being around successful people which expand me.

I welcome my desires changing, my expectations changing, my alignment changing as I become increasingly successful. I am still the same person as I was before. I am now a more expanded version of myself.

My power and success come from a place of love, a place of confidence and worth, a place of knowing. I am a good person who has worked for it, earned it, deserve it.

I become more of myself through success. I am an expanded version of myself.

My dreams become reality.

I create success easily and automatically.

I am loving and kind in my success. I am generous of heart and spirit with the addition of success and prosperity in my life.

I am changing into my best self. I am becoming someone that I like even more, and that others like even more. I am a success.

My fear of success is now dissolving completely.

I allow myself to step forward. I shine in my light. I am proud of who I am. I embrace all that I can, and I will be.

I am comfortable with being famous.

Any fear of lack of freedom that results from my fame and success is a price I am willing to pay. I let go of all fear surrounding my success.

I allow myself to flow with the ups and downs that come with my chosen passion and profession.

I acknowledge my skills, my talents, my dedication, my hard work, my commitment, my drive, my determination, and my discipline to my goal. I own and recognise my accomplishments proudly.

I believe that I am already successful.

I did this. I am successful. Me and only me. I deserve this. I earned it. I belong here in this success.

I am proud of what I have achieved. I worked for it. I deserve success.

Success makes my life better, more enriched, and more fulfilled.

Whatever I define success as, I align myself to it.

Success is in my world and life, now.

I am comfortable with success. I make friends with success. I believe that I deserve success. Success is showing up increasingly in my life.

I created many successes that are already in existence in my world. I see and recognise them all.

The more I focus on the successes that I already have, the more success I will create.

I see the small wins I have already created and achieved. I appreciate and value them. I appreciate and value myself for creating them.

The energy of my existing success is expanding now. More wins are already on their way to me.

More wins are showing up in my life and in my reality every day.

14

AFFIRMATIONS FOR A HEALTHY BODY

My body is in balance with well-being on every level: mind, body, spirit, emotions, energy, and vibration.

My body is the housing for my soul, my essence, my spirit, and my life-force. My body matters.

I desire a healthy and energised body.

I look after, love and protect my joints, organs, and systems.

I desire and align with good health to enable me to achieve my goals easily and comfortably.

I love and respect my body. I protect and nurture my body.

I eat the right food that was designed for my biological body, in the right quantities.

I enjoy and give my body healthy oils and plenty of water daily. I choose the right food to give me the energy and vitality to be well.

My body is an incredible force of creation. My body is a healing machine.

I remove stress from my life.

I move my body daily.

My body is repairing and resetting itself now.

My body is restoring itself to amazing, good health.

When my body is aching or in pain, I examine what I have done, or eaten. I find my answers and am easily able to make changes to support my body.

I am easily able to research the areas that are of relevance to me and my health.

I am easily able to change my way of eating and living to one that supports my body.

I eat natural, whole foods. I limit my exposure to high sugar foods. I avoid high carbohydrate food and grains.

I choose to eat single ingredient food.

I avoid sticky, starchy, processed foods. I know they harm my body. I love my body and choose wellness.

My body deserves all good things. My body deserves and desires my love, care, and protection.

I listen to my body, it tells me, it guides me.

My body wants to feel good. I love my body and I want my body to feel great.

I am what I eat. I eat wisely.

My body needs movement. I move my body daily in a way that works for me.

I reduce the stresses in my life in order to help my body be in balance and at peace.

I am living a healthy, pain free life.

I am living a life full of vitality. I have all the energy that I need to live life to its richest and fullest.

15

AFFIRMATIONS FOR LOVING CONNECTIONS

Loving connections are essential to my well-being. I embrace and welcome loving connections in my life.

I choose healthy, happy relationships and connections.

I choose relationships that help me to grow and be more of who I am.

I grow and thrive within society, communities, friendships, and relationships. I welcome social interaction with others.

I am open to increasing and expanding my insight, awareness, boundaries, patience, and forgiveness in all my relationships.

I love all of myself unconditionally.

My heart is open. I am open to my own love and access to all that I am and all that I can be.

I have the ability to connect with others. I am ready, willing, and able to connect from the heart and build loving, supportive relationships and friendships.

I treat myself with kindness. I honour, respect, and really love myself unconditionally.

I value and trust myself. I am trustworthy. I believe that people are trustworthy. I trust people.

I accept all of myself, exactly as I am, unconditionally.

I am reliable with myself. I honour my promises. If I promise myself something, I will do it.

I listen to myself. I listen to my inner voice, inner needs, desires and wants.

I am letting go of all my insecurities.

My heart is healed fully from all past hurts. I am healed emotionally from past wounds. Any wounds that remain I allow to pass through me easily and gently.

I am choosing to let go of all blocks to love.

I am choosing a new way of thinking in relationships.

My relationships going forward now reflect my true love and loyalty for myself.

It is now safe for me to love.

It is now safe for me to trust.

It is now safe for me to be vulnerable with the right person.

Most men and most women are incredibly loving. I am now aligning myself with those that love fully. I am aligned with true love, healthy love, beautiful love.

I forgive my past hurts and now align with my future loving connections.

I have amended my boundaries. I have pulled back from harmful commitments. I have reassessed my responsibilities. I have let go of the need for approval.

I am growing beautiful new relationships and improving the ones I already have.

I am building a more fulfilling, enriching life, connected life, for myself.

I believe that love is respect, care, trust, loyalty, honour, kindness, acceptance, openness, and vulnerability. I am aligned to all of these qualities and have them in abundance in my being.

Love is honest, open, accepting and kind.

I am my own best friend and treat myself the way that I would treat others.

I release all self-critical thought. I shower myself with love and praise.

I forgive myself for past self-criticism and condemning self-judgement.

I am loving myself. I am respecting myself. My relationships and connections mirror this back to me.

I am building loving, close connections with others.

AFFIRMATIONS FOR HAPPINESS

I am happy.

I am able to easily step into a state of happiness.

I value all positive, uplifting emotions.

I value happiness, serenity, calmness.

I am aligned with uplifting, energising emotions.

I embrace all emotions and recognise that they play their part in my overall wellbeing.

I experience joy often. Joy feels amazing. Joy is amazing. I love joy. I am aligned with joy.

I radiate out contentment and serenity. I am calm.

Positive emotions invoke in me a feeling of wellbeing. I am positive now.

I let go of the need to feel happy all the time. I value many other emotions that also help me feel good.

I am here to experience a myriad of emotions and feelings including that which is negative. I embrace them all.

I am letting go of the expectation to feel happy all of the time.

I am living life fully, with all its ups and downs.

I embrace contrast. Contrast helps me to know what I do and don't want. Contrast helps me to shift my thinking, desires, wants, and needs, and work towards that which I want. I value contrast.

I let go of the judgement of the emotions and feelings that make me feel bad or down. I let go of wanting, needing, expecting, to feel good all of the time. All emotions are valid.

I am allowing all feelings to be valid. I allow myself to feel good anyway, whatever emotions I am experiencing.

I am feeling good exactly where I am, wherever that may be. I let go of expecting to stay in happiness as a permanent state of being.

I accept that happiness is one of many emotions, and that all are valid, all are important, and all wish to be experienced by my soul.

I let go of the desire to chase happiness. I allow happy to come to me. I am a magnet for happiness.

I am a magnet for positive emotions.

I feel beautiful. I see the beauty in nature, in others, and in myself.

I connect with that which I wish to be. I feel the feeling of that which I am wanting to feel.

I am easily able to imagine the feeling I wish to feel and to step into it.

I am attracting happiness and other feel-good feelings into my world.

I am connected with happiness. I am connected to calmness, ease, contentment. I am connected to satisfaction, and all positive feelings.

I allow all good feelings into my world. I know and trust that more of the same is coming to me now.

PART 3 – RECEIVE

17

AFFIRMATIONS FOR KINDNESS

I love kindness. Kindness has a ripple effect which travels far. Kindness is contagious. Kindness is infectious and spreads like wildfire. I love to be kind.

I am kind.

I show kindness to as many people as possible.

Kindness creates a wave of loving energy, both within me and within its recipient. I love being kind.

I step into kindness now. Kindness is uplifting, inspiring, validating, harmonious and powerful.

All acts of kindness, big and small, are valid. I am kind, always.

I choose kindness. I impact the individual and the collective with my kindness.

I perform a random act of kindness every day.

I spread kindness in my daily life.

My kindness impacts the soul and the light in the recipient I am being kind to.

I assist the collective in my kindness.

I give kindness freely and lovingly, unconditionally, and lovingly. I let go of expecting or needing thanks. My kindness is a free gift.

I perform acts of kindness because it feels right, because I can, because I want to. I want to be kind, always.

My soul reaches out to another soul in distress, desiring to help. I listen, and act with kindness.

Kindness grows me, expands my love, my light, and my happiness. I grow in kindness every day.

I feel good when I do good. I love to do good.

I am aligned with kindness and go about performing random acts of kindness on and for others.

I am abundant in kindness. I am unlimited in my kindness.

I am aligning with all that I want to be. I choose to be kind. I look for opportunities to be kind in my everyday life. I am open to opportunities to be and show kindness every day.

I am more happy, more joyful, more loving, more fulfilled, and more enriched when I show kindness.

I am in alignment with receiving by giving. I am giving and gifting kindness.

Kindness comes back to me, ten-fold. My life and world are increasingly kind.

I am open to receiving kindness from others, always.

18

AFFIRMATIONS FOR GRATITUDE

I feel the vibration of my words and my feelings. I am aligned with my feelings and my vibration.

I am so happy and grateful now that all good things come to me. I feel these words, I express fully my gratitude for all good things with energy and feeling.

I am so happy and thankful for my life.

I am grateful for ease. I am grateful for peace. I am grateful for freedom.

I see and feel the gratitude for everything I receive and everything I have. I am aligned with receiving wonderful things and experiences.

I am so grateful for the money in my wallet.

I allow myself to become one with gratitude. More wonderful things to be grateful for are showing up for me every day.

I start my day with gratitude. I end my day with gratitude. I am so grateful.

I am so happy and grateful that I had a great night's sleep.

I am so happy and grateful that I have a job.

I am grateful that I am retired.

I am grateful for my clothes.

I am grateful for my water, shower, bath that enables me to feel clean and refreshed.

I am grateful for my health.

I am grateful for my food.

I am grateful for my transport that enable me to get to where I need to get to, with ease.

I am grateful for my family and friends.

I am grateful for my heating, my air conditioning, my physical comfort.

I notice what I can I be grateful for today and I am grateful.

I am already in a vibration of gratitude and at one with gratitude.

I live in an attitude of gratitude from a place of now, from a place of power and from a place of love. I am gratitude.

I create an attitude of gratitude in my everyday life.

More goodness, joy, and things to be grateful for show up for me every day. I am so grateful.

I am so blessed and grateful for it all.

19

AFFIRMATIONS FOR FORGIVENESS

I choose forgiveness. I have the power to choose to forgive. I choose forgiveness.

Forgiveness grows me in compassion, empathy, and sympathy, understanding and tolerance. I love to forgive.

I am patient and accepting. I am merciful. I am gracious.

I grow in my awareness and self-love through forgiveness. I grow in my own peace and serenity. I grow in my power to be non-judgemental. Forgiveness is an act of love for self and for the other. I forgive all. I choose forgiveness.

The bigger and the more powerful the perceived wrong is, the bigger the growth opportunity is for my soul. I am able to forgive, easily. I am open to opportunities for growth on all levels. I am releasing old hurts and unforgiveness now.

Forgiveness serves me and helps my personal power, maturity, wisdom, resilience, flexibility, and my inner peace. I choose my own inner peace over the anger and hostility I felt to the other.

I am healing, releasing, and rebalancing.

I am growing in light, in love and in peace.

I forgive. I am freeing myself from the heavy energies of unforgiveness.

I am stepping into my power and freedom to create the world and the life that I want through forgiveness.

It is time to let go. It is time to forgive. I forgive all and everything that ever harmed me. I am aligned with letting go and forgiving all.

I allow myself to step into forgiveness. It frees me. It liberates me. It benefits me.

I forgive myself unconditionally for all that I have judged in myself and my actions to be wrong.

I am choosing to forgive those that have wronged me.

I am freeing myself from past resentments. I forgive all who have hurt me.

I align myself with forgiveness and peace now.

I am commanding all that is not love within me to dissolve. I step into forgiveness for all.

I am freeing myself now from all past pains and forgive all involved.

I am calling upon the Angelic Realms to assist me in my expansion of forgiveness. Thank you for helping me to forgive this person for their actions. Thank you for helping me to be compassionate and tolerant.

I am calling on my I AM. Thank you for helping me to let go of my judgement of others and their actions.

I let go of the thinking that some deeds are unforgivable. All is forgivable when I choose to align with it. I choose forgiveness now.

I forgive myself.

I am at peace within myself. I am love. I am compassion. I am tolerant and patient.

I see the way that life improves for me once I forgive. I choose forgiveness now.

20

AFFIRMATIONS FOR ACCEPTANCE AND FLOW

I let go of resistance of that which I perceive to be wrong.

I allow myself to let go and let God.

I allow myself to flow in harmony with the universe and life.

I embrace change when life is flowing towards it.

Acceptance is ease. I see what is happening as an energy of flow. I work with the flow. I come to terms with it easily and gently. I accept it.

I allow life to be what it is.

I trust that life is helping me move to something better when it no longer flows well. I trust in life.

I accept the consequences of the results of necessary change in a productive, harmonious way. I am in acceptance of what is.

I trust that my inner being is protecting and helping me by removing a situation from my life. I accept it easily.

Some change is uncomfortable for me. I let go of resistance and go with the flow. I step into acceptance and release discomfort.

I may not know why something is changing, but I accept it anyway. I trust, that in time, the benefits will be shown.

I go with the flow of life and trust that it is all working out exactly the right way for me, right now.

Life moves in rhythms, phases, periods, and begins again with something new. I accept that things end and begin again in a different form. I embrace the new.

I am in the flow of life and accept what is.

Life always works out for me.

I accept that I create all change at some level. I create change because my inner being asks for change. I accept this and take responsibility and ownership of this. I release resistance.

I am living the life that is right for me, good for me, aligned with me, and everything flows and flows well.

I trust that all change is for my betterment, for my growth, for me. I trust this, know this, feel this, align with this. My life now works better and better for me.

In my acceptance of what is, is my receiving. I receive peace, serenity, hopefulness, trust. I trust in life, I trust in change, I accept it all. Life is unfolding more into its richest form. It does this for me.

21

AFFIRMATIONS FOR VISUALISATION

My mind is incredibly powerful. My mind is capable of magnificent imagination. What I can imagine, I can create into reality through the power of my visualisation.

I imagine my most ideal life and what it looks like, what it feels like. I feel it, I step into it. I feel it. I feel the emotion of it.

I am unlimited. I am free of all restrictions.

I am lovable.

I deserve all good things.

I am now creating the life that I dream of.

All that I desire is on its way to me now.

I trust in life. I trust myself. I trust and know that I am creating the life I was meant to live and be the person I was meant to be.

I am fulfilling my potential, now.

I easily visualise my ideal life. I feel the feelings of that which I imagine.

I think it, I visualise it, I feel it.

I vibrate at the correctly aligned vibrational resonance that matches my goals.

I visualise my goals. I align with my goals. I feel the feelings of having my goals, now.

I am now attracting that which I want through visualising and feeling that which I desire.

I use my powerful and vivid imagination to create my most wonderful reality.

22

AFFIRMATIONS FOR ALIGNING WITH GOALS

I bring into reality my dreams, goals, and aspirations. I am aligned with them fully.

Every part of me is in vibrational agreement with that which I want to have.

I have identified my goals. I am clear in my vision of my goals. I feel the feelings of having achieved my goals.

I am clear in my goal.

I put all my focus and all my energy into my goal. I am clear on it.

I am disciplined with my goal.

I have researched my goal. I know what to do to bring it into reality. I act to achieve my goal.

I have given my goal a timeframe. I have given my goal time, attention, care, and love. My goal is now on its way.

I am committed to my goal. I am willing and able to learn about my goal.

I am willing to learn new skills and educate myself on the subject of my goal.

I am willing and able to dedicate time to my goal in order to achieve it.

I do whatever I need to do to put myself in alignment with my goal and give myself the time to do it, within my highest good.

I set my goals in an achievable timeframe. I move towards it beautifully in divine timing.

All parts of me are in agreement with the having, the obtaining and the securing, of my goal.

I allow resistance and fear to my goal to come forward. I easily, gently resolve resistance to my goal. I am easily able to negotiate with my resistance. I reassure resistance and release it easily.

I feel into my goal. I ask my entire being, are we ready, are we good, do we all want this, and I listen to the answers. When I feel resistance, I invite all that is not in agreement with my goal to come forward for resolution, without blame, shame, or judgement, but with acceptance, love and understanding.

I am easily able to move from reluctance into agreement, when my goal is within my highest good.

I am fully aligned with my greatest life and my goals in life.

I energetically move forward towards my goal.

I am taking inspired action and willing to do what is necessary to bring all parts of me into alignment with my goal.

I am now fully in alignment with that which I desire.

23

AFFIRMATIONS FOR OPPORTUNITIES

I am called to action. I am open to inspiration. I am open to new ideas.

I allow my intuition to guide me forward, step by step, towards my goals.

The Universe rearranges itself, people, places, situations, and opportunities to bring me further into alignment with my goals. I trust this and go with the flow of new opportunities.

I allow and am aware of the signs and synchronicities around me. I allow life to flow for me.

I know that perceived accidents and coincidences are the universes way of guiding me. I am open to guidance from within.

I allow the signs and synchronicities to be my light, lighting my way to where I really want to be.

I look for the flow in my life. I see the signs, the synchronicities. I am aware of and open to opportunities.

I act on the small nudges from inside. I pay attention to the signs, and I trust them.

I allow my soul, my being, my God-force, my I AM, to guide me, to lead the way, and I follow. I follow willingly.

I am thankful and grateful that the universe and life is assisting me onto my right path.

I am releasing restrictive conditions upon my goals and dreams.

I trust that life will move me into exactly the right place, at the right time.

I trust in serendipity and know the universe is rearranging itself to support me. I align myself with this.

I allow life to move me where it knows it is best for me, in perfect timing, to the perfect place.

The Universe is working with me, moving me gently into my best life.

I allow myself to be flexible with my goal. I trust that the universe will bring me it, or something better. I am always open to something better.

I allow my inner voice, my intuition, my internal sat-nav, my higher self, my vibration, my goals, wishes and dreams, to signal me, and I listen. I allow.

I am so grateful for the opportunities that life is presenting to me right now.

24

AFFIRMATIONS FOR RECEIVING

I am now fully in the receiving of all that I desire. It is here, now. I feel it, I know it. I am aligned, I am ready, now!

I am in my full power.

I energise my goals with focused intent.

I easily clear out old belief systems that do not serve me.

I recognise my importance.

I align all parts of myself and believe that all is possible, achievable, and attainable.

I now actively encourage and praise myself, often.

I totally believe that I can achieve my goals.

I am now living my life in a way that feels right to me.

I let go easily of others' opinions, thoughts, distractions, and negativity.

I am now living in a higher vibration, tuned in, and working with my higher self, soul, intuition, energy, and Source to create my best life.

I am now in full alignment with my goals.

I am always creating; constantly, consistently, absolutely, and always. I am now creating an abundant, joyous life.

I am light. I am love. I am a spark of consciousness that separated from Source. I will return to Source, expanded. I am Source personified, glorified, and much revered.

I deserve all good things.

I am now able to align my thoughts and beliefs to serve me and support me.

I am open to the signs, synchronicities and serendipitous events, opportunities and options that are being created for me by the Universe. I am open to receive.

I am in awe of how the Universe rearranges itself. I have such love and respect for the Universe.

Love is in and all around me, always. I am automatically bringing more love into my life, including a life I love.

I am a spark of consciousness, I am love, I am truth, I am magnificent.

I stand fully in my power, in my light, in my truth, always.

I AM ALL THAT I AM.

I AM manifesting all of my dreams, my goals, and my desires, easily.

I AM my best version of myself, now.

I AM creating my greatest life, now!

I AM ready, now!

I am much loved, eternally.

THE END